Writing at Work

A Quick and Easy Guide to Grammar and Effective Business Writing

Ellis Morgan

DORMOUSE

Published in the United Kingdom by Dormouse Press,
an imprint of Guidemark Publishing Limited

ISBN 978-0-9569466-2-1

www.dormousepress.co.uk

Writing at Work

A Quick and Easy Guide to Grammar
and Effective Business Writing

Communicating effectively at work

If you want to communicate effectively at work, you have to be able to write straightforward, easy to read letters, emails, reports, and leaflets. Good communication is an essential part of building a successful business—it can really set you apart from your competitors.

Writing well at work means understanding your target audience and pitching your language and tone of voice to suit your readers. Try to keep things simple. Don't be one of those people who use long words and complex sentence structures in the mistaken belief that it makes them sound intelligent. Every office has someone like that—they churn out complicated reports that are so boring that people abandon them half way through; and their emails are so difficult to understand they fail to deliver their message. That isn't good writing. If you're guilty of pretentious prose, I suggest you give yourself a good talking to—now! And then carry on reading this book.

It's organised as an A to Z guide and includes answers to some of the most frequently asked questions about language and grammar, plus useful tips for effective business writing. There's also advice on using straightforward language to make your business documents easier to read and understand, and a list of everyday alternatives to some of the trickiest words.

This is a practical and easy guide to business writing, not a comprehensive guide to grammar or punctuation (if it sparks your interest in language, I'd encourage you to read more on the subject—see page 129). You can also get help from the Plain English Campaign's website at www.plainenglish.co.uk. The organisation has been campaigning against jargon, gobbledygook and misleading public information since 1979.

Once you've finished reading your copy of *Writing at Work*, keep it on your desk and refer to it whenever you need to. As you learn more about language, your confidence as a writer will grow and your need for this book will diminish.

Remember though that none of us are perfect. Even the most experienced writers and communicators have to refer to a dictionary or grammar guide from time to time. Occasionally they even make mistakes!

Don't expect to get it right first time

Don't be afraid of language. If you're asked to write a report, a letter, or the wording for a leaflet, take a deep breath and tackle it one word at a time. Start at the beginning and keep going to the end. Or start in the middle, if you prefer. Whatever you feel most comfortable with.

Don't expect to get things right first time. The challenge of writing any document can be intimidating, especially if you think you've got to sit down and instantly compose beautiful, flowing sentences with perfect spelling and grammar. Thankfully, that's not how things work. Even the best writers in the world have to edit their manuscripts—finely tuned editing makes for good writing.

So what's the best way to tackle a writing project? Let's say you've been asked to write a report. Begin by asking yourself what you need to say. Who is it you're writing to? What is the message you want to convey? Are you writing to inform, advise, or persuade? Jot down some subject headings and make notes. If your company has a standard template for business reports, use it to structure your document.

Business reports usually start with an **introduction**, which should include the subject and aims of the report—in other words, what you're reporting on or evaluating, and why. The next section is the **background** or **overview**, which will include information that puts the report into context. You might also want to include a political, economic, social, and technological (PEST) analysis in this section of the report, and outline the methodology you've used to carry out any research.

Next is the **main body** of the report, which should feature all of the headings you noted earlier. Use this section to outline key issues and ideas and include statistics or other data to illustrate or explain your points.

Finally, summarise your analysis of the issues you've raised by pulling together the main points of the report and giving your **conclusions** or **recommendations**.

'Ok,' you say, 'that sounds fairly straightforward. But how do I put all the words together? How do I know what to *say*?'

The best approach is to imagine that a good friend has walked into your office and is sitting next to you at your desk. 'Hi,' they say, 'I hear you've been asked to write a report. What's it about?'

How would you respond? What would you say? Hold on... don't tell me... write down your answer instead. Type out the things you would say to your friend and you'll have the beginnings of your report. It doesn't matter how clumsy the words may sound at this stage; you can always go back and make changes later. At least now you have something to build on. Keep in mind the well known saying among writers: *you can't edit a blank page*. The important thing is to make a start; unless you do, you'll never get that report finished.

Once you've completed your first draft, go back to the beginning and start to edit. Cut out any repetition and check that you've included all of the relevant facts. You should also check your spelling and grammar at this stage and make sure the layout of the document is clear and consistent. If there's time, ask a colleague to look at your report—and don't be defensive if they make suggestions on how it can be improved.

Finally, once you've made your changes, read through the report one last time, double checking that you've covered all of the points and headings you noted when you started out. Refer to your copy of *Writing at Work* if you need to check any points of grammar or language. When you're happy that it does what it needs to do, send it out.

Writing a report or any other document doesn't have to be an ordeal. All you have to do is sit down and make a start.

Writing at Work

A to Z

ABBREVIATIONS AND ACRONYMS

Abbreviations and acronyms are useful sometimes. They can save you having to repeat a long phrase or lengthy product name in full—but there are rules about the best way to use them. Before we talk about the rules though, let's be clear about what abbreviations and acronyms are.

Abbreviations are spoken as letters—VIP, PTO, and CCTV for example. Acronyms are letters that can be spoken as a word, such as NATO, UNESCO or NIMBY.

Most of us use our own abbreviations and acronyms in the workplace; in meetings, in conversations and when we write. It's easy to assume that everyone knows what they stand for, but that's not always the case. The best way to deal with acronyms or abbreviations in written documents is to put the name or phrase in full when you first mention it, followed immediately by the abbreviation or acronym in round brackets.

Example: *The Electronic Testing Widget (ETW) was used to scan a range of new products.*

After that, it's ok to use the abbreviation or acronym on its own. If you're writing a long document or using an abbreviation on a website, it's a good idea to repeat the full version of the acronym or abbreviation on each new page. And remember that some general abbreviations like BBC and NHS are familiar to everyone, so it's fine to use them without any explanation.

ADJECTIVES

Adjectives are words that describe things. They can also modify nouns and pronouns. Their function is to add colour and clarity by providing extra detail.

Example (adjectives underlined): *It was a <u>boring</u> game full of <u>clumsy</u> errors.*

ADVERBS

Adverbs are closely related to adjectives but whereas adjectives modify nouns and pronouns, adverbs describe or modify verbs and adjectives, and even other adverbs.

Examples (adverbs underlined):

The dog barked <u>loudly</u> (used to modify a verb)

The dog barked for <u>almost</u> an hour (used to modify an adjective)

The dog barked <u>very</u> loudly (adverb modifying another adverb)

APOSTROPHES

Apostrophes are used in a number of ways—to show where a word has been shortened (known as a contraction—see page 21), and to show possession (to indicate when something belongs to something). Using apostrophes to show possession can be a troublesome area of grammar, so here's a quick guide to how it should be done.

With plural or singular nouns that don't end with the letter 's', simply add an apostrophe and an 's'.

Example: *the cat's whiskers, or the children's play area.*

For **plural nouns** that end with an 's', add the apostrophe only.

Example: *The members' conference.*

When you're dealing with **singular nouns** that end with an 's' you can either add an apostrophe, or an apostrophe and an 's'.

Example: *Mrs Jones's house or Mrs Jones' house; James's car or James' car; the actress's dress or the actress' dress.*

These are all acceptable, because all the nouns end in 's'.

You shouldn't use apostrophes for plurals such as *my files*, *her DVDs*, or *the 1980s*, or when '*its*' is used to show possession, rather than as an abbreviation for 'it is' (see Its or It's on page 42).

And finally, don't make the classic mistake seen so often on shop signs and in newspaper adverts: *Half price blouse's* or *Potato's - 95p a kilo*. There should be no apostrophe in either of these adverts, and the plural of potato is potatoes.

ASTERISK*

These are used to draw special attention to a section of information within your text. They are often used with special offers to make people aware that 'terms and conditions apply'.

*If you insert an asterisk don't forget to include an explanation somewhere on the page.

B

BULLET POINTS

Bullet points are great for presenting a list of items or highlighting key points in a document—but don't overuse them. A text peppered with bullet points will quickly lose its flow.

In Microsoft Word, you have a choice of bullet points ranging from standard circle-shaped bullets, through to arrows, ticks or any other shape you choose to define yourself. My advice is to stick to traditional bullet points, unless you've got a really good reason not to.

The rules for using bullet points depend on whether you're listing short items or complete sentences.

In the case of **short items**, if each item has fewer than six words and isn't a complete sentence, your bullet points should be in lower case and have no punctuation at the end of the lines, except on the last line, which should end in a full stop. Confused? Take a look at the example and all will become clear.

Example:

There are advantages to using bullet points. They:

- are easy to read
- help break up the text
- list things clearly
- vary the page layout.

When it comes to **complete sentences**, treat longer bullet points as full sentences. Start each one with a capital letter and end each one with a full stop. Don't forget to make sure that the wording of your bullet points matches your opening phrase.

Example:

Spell checking your document is important because:

- Misspelt words make you look unprofessional and reflect badly on your organisation.

- It helps to make sure you're communicating the right message to the person reading the document.

- Typos can be unintentionally humorous or, worse, insulting, so it's best to avoid them.

BE BOLD

Using a **bold** font is a great way to highlight key words and phrases, or to make headings stand out. This is a much better method of drawing attention to text and headings than underlining or using block capitals, which are particularly hard for people with a visual impairment to read.

Don't be too 'bold' though. It should be the key words and phrases you aim to highlight. Too many bold words will dilute the impact.

C

CONTRACTIONS

For a less formal style, write to your readers as you would talk to them. Use 'we're' instead of 'we are' and 'I'll' rather than 'I will'. This is what you'd say if you spoke to someone face-to-face or over the phone, so why not use the same language when you write to them?

Contractions use an apostrophe to show where a letter or letters have been left out: 'you've' for 'you have' and 'there's' for 'there is', for example. The quickest way to check whether your contraction is correct is to say the words in full without the contraction.

Example:

You're welcome (you are welcome). ✓

Your welcome. ✗

This style of writing is friendly and ideal for use in newsletters and leaflets, but avoid using contractions if you're writing a formal or legal document, or if you're writing to someone whose first language isn't English.

CONJUNCTIONS

These are the words that link two nouns, phrases, and other parts of a sentence together. Conjunctions are words such as: *and, if, for, at, but, so, as, yet, or.*

Example:

Jim is a specialist in sales <u>and</u> marketing.

Jim enjoys sales <u>but</u> prefers to work in marketing.

CLICHÉS

We're all guilty of using clichés from time to time. They're phrases that start out as a new expression—a way of saying something that's novel, neat or amusing—but over time the phrase gets used so often it becomes stale and unoriginal.

It's tempting to use clichés when we're feeling a bit lazy or inarticulate. They do have their uses sometimes, and there's nothing fundamentally wrong with them. Just don't use them too often.

Examples:

- *At the end of the day.*

- *Can of worms.*

- *Catch 22 situation.*

- *Handle with kid gloves.*

- *Light at the end of the tunnel.*

- *Working in the dark.*

- *All things being equal.*

There you have it. Remember, when it comes to clichés, avoid them like the plague.

CAPITAL LETTERS

Use capitals if you're referring to something specific, but not if you're referring to something general.

Examples:

(**specific**): *I asked Dr Brown for a repeat prescription.*

(**general**): *I asked the doctor for a repeat prescription.*

(**specific**): *Tom was a student at Oxford University.*

(**general**): *Tom was in his second year at university.*

The other thing to remember is to be cautious about using block capitals in the main text of your document AS THESE CAN BE REALLY DIFFICULT TO READ, especially for people who are visually impaired. People don't read words letter by letter, but by recognising the overall shape of the word. A mixture of upper and lower case letters will provide the reader with visual clues and make the words quicker to read. Having said that, there are times when capital letters can be useful to draw attention to words, or to emphasise text. The section headings in this book are all capitals, and many posters and signs often make use of capital letters. Avoid using them too often though because they can make you look LIKE YOU'RE SHOUTING!

D

DATES

The clearest way to display dates is to write them simply as 9 January, 31 August, or 17 December. There's no need to include the letters 'st', 'nd', 'rd' or 'th'. If you do include these letters, it's likely that your word processor will change them to a small superscript font (9th January, 31st August and 17th December), which break up the flow of the text and aren't so easy to read.

Avoid referring to dates in numerical date formats (set out as DD-MM-YYYY). These look awkward, but there's also another problem with them. In the US they are set out differently (as MM-DD-YYYY), which could lead to confusion. 04/06/2011 in the UK would refer to 4 June 2011. In the US, the same date would refer to 6 April 2011.

DIRECT YOUR READER

If you want the person reading your letter or document to do something, then tell them! In business terms, this is known as a 'call to action'. You might want to prompt them to visit your website, call your enquiry line, complete a form, or place an order.

Be clear about any instructions you give. If you want your customer to complete a form and return it to you, say so. Don't be vague.

Example:

Avoid: *Forms should be returned to My Company, 123 High Street, Anytown, AB1 2CD.*

Better: *Please fill in this form and return it in the envelope provided to My Company, 123 High Street, Anytown, AB1 2CD.*

Including a 'call to action' at the end of your text can really improve the effectiveness of your letter or leaflet.

ELLIPSIS...

You've probably noticed the use of three full stops in a row, but may not be aware that they're called 'ellipsis.' The use of an ellipsis in writing indicates missing words that aren't essential, an unfinished thought, or words that the reader is expected to know.

Examples:

We don't want the children to have to miss school... we can arrange our trip around the school holidays.

In the example above, ellipsis are used to show a slight pause. An alternative would be to split the sentence in two.

'I wonder what will happen if I pull this lever...'

In this example we're left wondering whether the lever was pulled or not and what happened if it was.

He started singing the British National Anthem: 'God save our gracious Queen...'

Here, the ellipsis is used to indicate that the sentence or words continue, even though only the opening portion is shown.

Chances are, you're unlikely to need ellipsis in business writing, but at least you now know what they're used for.

EVERYDAY ENGLISH

When you're writing, avoid using words that you wouldn't use in everyday conversation. Sometimes you'll need to be formal, especially if you're writing a technical or legal document, but generally you should choose words that are as short, clear and straightforward as possible.

If you were talking to someone would you say: '*The contract commenced in November and will conclude in February*'? No? Didn't think so. So why use that kind of language in a document? Instead write: '*The contract started in November and will end in February*'.

Using **everyday English** will make your documents

less formal, more readable, and easier to understand. You can also save money by writing internal documents in everyday English—on average documents written using straightforward English take staff around 30% less time to read. For a list of everyday words, turn to page 105.

ETC ETC

When you use Latin words in English you're assuming that your reader knows what they mean and, the truth is, not everyone does. Latin also makes things doubly hard for people whose first language isn't English.

It's better to cut Latin phrases out of your text and replace them with a straightforward English word. Here are some of the most commonly used Latin words and phrases, alongside English alternatives.

Examples:

bona fide: genuine
eg (exampli gratia): for example, such as
etc (et cetera): and so on
ie (id est): that is
NB (nota bene): please note
per: each, a
per se: as such
pro rata: in proportion
via: by way of

F

FEWER OR LESS

Fewer should be used when you refer to people or things in the plural (things that can be counted). Less should be used to refer to things that can't be counted or with singular nouns (such as bread, money and time).

Examples:

Helen should drink less alcohol, or
Helen should drink fewer glasses of wine.

The shop sold less bread this week, or
The shop sold fewer loaves of bread this week.

Less adults were in the audience during the matinee performance. ✗

Fewer adults were in the audience during the matinee performance. ✓

FONT

Choose a font that is clear, easy to read and suitable for how your words will be published. For short business documents use plainer fonts, known as sans serif (which means they don't have any stylised curves or variations in line thickness). **Arial** is a popular choice and is available on most PCs. Used at a minimum size 11 or, even better 12, it's ideal for word processed documents and presentations.

Serif fonts are considered easier to read in longer printed documents and are generally used by newspapers, magazines and book publishers. This book, for example, is printed using a serif font.

When it comes to websites, most use sans serif fonts, because they are modern and considered easier to read on low resolution computer screens.

A warning about some of the *fancier fonts* available on your PC, particularly the *script fonts*. These can be difficult to read, especially for people whose first language isn't English and those with poor levels of literacy.

Most companies will have a particular font they use in professionally produced leaflets and brochures. Again, these are usually chosen for their readability and clarity. If you have a design or marketing team, talk to them about when these should be used.

G

GRAMMAR

Adopting a less formal writing style will give your letters, leaflets and newsletters a friendly tone of voice, but that doesn't mean your writing should be sloppy or contain grammatical errors.

One of the first rules of grammar is that subject and verb must agree, both in person and number. Here's what that means in simple terms.

Examples:

A singular subject needs a singular verb:
Julie <u>is</u> happy.

A plural or compound subject needs a plural verb:
Julie and Stuart <u>are</u> happy.

A first person subject needs a verb in the first person:
I am happy.

A third person subject needs a verb in the third person:
She is happy.

Sounds simple, right? Well, not always. Applying the rule can sometimes take a little extra thought. For instance, it can be difficult to identify which word or phrase is the subject of a sentence. A subject can sometimes be separated from the verb by an intervening phrase, but this shouldn't affect the number of the verb.

Example:

Here the **subject** is *purpose*, the **intervening phrase** is *of his visits* and the **verb** is *was.*

*The **purpose** of his visits **was** to boost morale.* ✔

*The **purpose** of his visits **were** to boost morale.* ✗

It's easy to work out whether you've got it right by removing the intervening phrase:

The purpose was to boost morale. ✔

The purpose were to boost morale. ✗

Once you've identified the subject in your sentence, it's usually pretty easy to work out what the number of the verb should be. Let's clarify with another example.

Example:

*The **collection** of rare stamps **was** sold at auction.* ✓

*The **collection** of rare stamps **were** sold at auction.* ✗

We can check this by removing the **intervening phrase** *of rare stamps*:

The collection was sold at auction. ✓

The collection were sold at auction. ✗

Another thing to avoid is the use of something called **misplaced modifiers**. The secret to dealing with these is to keep related words together in the order that gives them the meaning you intend.

Example:

She almost lost all of the money.

She lost almost all of the money.

Both of these are grammatically correct, but each has a different meaning. What is it you want to say? In the first example, none of the money was lost. In the second, most of it was. If you get it wrong and misplace modifiers, you end up with a badly constructed sentence that doesn't say what you want it to. You're also in danger of confusing or unintentionally amusing your readers.

Example:

The patient's wound was dressed to avoid any more blood being lost by the nurse.

It isn't the nurse who's bleeding, so the sentence would be better written as: *The patient's wound was dressed by the nurse to avoid him losing any more blood.*

Or, even better: *The nurse dressed the patient's wound to avoid him losing more blood.*

Groucho Marx famously highlighted this problem in the film *Animal Crackers*, when he said:

"One morning I shot an elephant in my pajamas. How he got into my pajamas, I don't know."

To discuss English grammar thoroughly would require a much bigger book than this, and I want this to be a quick guide. However, if you're interested in learning more about how language works and the finer points of English grammar, check out the recommended books in the *Further Reading* section on page 129.

HYPHENS

These days, hyphens are used less often in standard text, but are still used in the following ways:

If a word already has a meaning without the hyphen

Example: *Re-cover* (meaning to cover again), as opposed to *recover* (to get better).

To avoid confusion

Examples: *Exotic-fish keeper* (a keeper of exotic fish, rather than a fish keeper who is exotic), *diabetic-nurse* (a nurse who takes care of diabetic patients, not a nurse who is diabetic), and a *hot-water engineer* (an engineer who looks after hot water systems, not a water engineer who is hot!).

For clarity

You can use hyphens to make odd-looking words clearer, usually where there is a clash of the same letter or vowels.

Examples: *Shell-like* (rather than shelllike), pre-empt (instead of preempt), and *co-operate* (cooperate).

With prefixes

Hyphens are also used with certain prefixes.

Examples: *Ante* (ante-natal) or *self* (self-employed).

HELP ACCESSING INFORMATION

If you're sending a document to a customer who has a visual impairment, it's good practice to offer to send them the text in large print or another format such as audio or Braille.

Large print documents should be typed at a minimum 16 point font, and ideally, 20. A quick and easy way to enlarge an A4 letter is to print it out as normal and then enlarge it on a photocopier to an A3 size. You can search online for organisations that will provide you with a Braille and audio transcription service. You might also need to search for translation services if you're asked to provide a document in another language.

I AND ME

The best way to check whether you should be using 'I' or 'me' in your sentence is to delete the other person from the sentence, or split it into two separate ones. If what you're left with makes sense, you know you've got it right.

Example one:

Henry and me aren't going to the party. ✗

Henry isn't going to the party. ✓

Me isn't going to the party. ✗

In this example the sentence should read:

Henry and I aren't going to the party. ✓

I am not going to the party. ✓

Example two:

The car wouldn't start, leaving Chris and I no alternative but to catch the bus. ✗

The car wouldn't start, leaving Chris no alternative but to catch the bus. ✓

The car wouldn't start, leaving I no alternative but to catch the bus. ✗

Which means this example should read:

The car wouldn't start, leaving Chris and me no alternative but to catch the bus. ✓

The car wouldn't start, leaving me no alternative but to catch the bus. ✓

ITS OR IT'S

Lots of people get confused about whether to use its or it's. It all depends on whether you're using the words to show possession or to abbreviate *it is*.

Use an apostrophe to show when you are contracting *it is*. The easiest way to check if you need the apostrophe is to put the missing letters back in to confirm whether or not it's really a contraction.

Examples:

It's a long way to Edinburgh from here.

It is a long way to Edinburgh from here. ✓

By introducing this new policy it's hoped that we can improve performance by 20%.

By introducing this new policy it is hoped that we can improve performance by 20%. ✓

The dog wagged it's tail and barked.

The dog wagged it is tail and barked. ✗

This should read:

The dog wagged its tail and barked.✓

'Its' as a possessive pronoun needs no apostrophe.

Examples:

The college encouraged its employees to learn new skills.

The bird stretched its wings and flew away.

You can find out more about the company by visiting its website.

J

JARGON

Every business organisation has its own jargon. Jargon is the shorthand language that we use in meetings or when we're talking to colleagues. Using jargon can be a positive thing as long as the people you're talking to understand what it means.

You shouldn't use jargon when you're writing to customers, or if you're writing to another business that isn't familiar with your company's unique terminology. Instead, explain things in simple terms.

Bear in mind that when new staff join your team, they won't be familiar with your company jargon, but they may be too embarrassed to say so. Help them along by explaining any jargon you use, at least until they've learned it for themselves.

K

KEEP IT CONSISTENT

Once you've decided on a writing style, make sure you maintain it. Adopt the same tone of voice throughout your document and once you've chosen a format for a particular phrase, use it consistently. For example, if you decide to write the phrase *anti social behaviour* without hyphens, don't write *anti-social behaviour* elsewhere in the same leaflet or letter. If you refer to an *employee toolkit* in one paragraph, don't change it to *employee tool kit* in the next. Once you've opted for one style, stick with it.

Keep your text layout consistent by maintaining the same size and format for headings and, unless there's a good reason, use the same font throughout the document.

KNOWLEDGE

Make sure you know your subject thoroughly before you start writing. Apply that knowledge but remember to make things clear for the reader, checking any facts you're unsure of. This is particularly important if you're producing a leaflet that will be printed and distributed widely. It's also wise to get someone else to check the text before you go to print (see Proof Reading on page 67).

L

LONG WORDS AND LONG SENTENCES

Why use a long word when a short one will do? Using long words may sound impressive, but they can be a hindrance when it comes to communicating clearly in writing. Why say 'subsequently' when 'later' is so much easier to understand? Wouldn't it be better to say 'often' instead of 'frequently'? The test is to ask yourself whether you'd use a word in conversation with your friends or colleagues.

For instance, would you honestly say: *'I frequently go to the gym'*? Wouldn't you be more likely to say: *'I often go to the gym'*?

Try to avoid **long sentences**. Aim for an average sentence length of between 15 and 20 words, with a maximum of 35 words. Anything longer and you're in danger of confusing or losing your reader.

You can reduce your sentence length by looking out

for linking words such as 'and' and 'but' and splitting the sentence into two. Or you could use bullet points instead.

That said, there is a place for long words and sentences. If you're writing to someone who is technically savvy, familiar with specialist terms, and fully understands the subject you are writing about, then it's fine to construct complex sentences and use longer words. Writing well is about adopting a style that suits your audience (see R for Reader on page 75).

LESS IS MORE

Don't overload your text with too much information. Trying to tell your reader everything in one go can be confusing. Keep things clear and simple—and direct them to your website to read further details if they need to.

LIE OR LAY?

These two words often trip people up, but once you learn their true meaning it's easy to understand which to use. Lay means to put or set something down. Lie means to recline or speak untruthfully.

Here the word 'lie' is used as a **verb**:

Examples:

He decided to lie on the bed and take a rest.

The woman can't be trusted. She often lies, especially about her age.

Use 'lie' or 'lies' as a **noun** when you're using it to explain untruths or false stories.

Example:

The excuse he was giving was clearly a lie.

Use the words, 'lay' or 'laid' as a **verb** when you want to describe something as being placed or arranged.

Examples:

She fainted, so he picked her up and lay her on the couch.

'Lay down your weapon,' shouted the police officer.

The brown chicken would always lay its eggs in the barn.

He laid the table for dinner, then went to lie down for a nap.

You can also use **'lay'** as an **adjective** when you want to refer to someone as an amateur or non-professional.

Example: *The lay preacher spoke to the congregation for almost an hour.*

M

MEANINGLESS PHRASES

There are lots of old fashioned phrases that still creep in to twenty first century business documents. Most of them are totally meaningless and sound like they were written a hundred years ago. Things like:

Please contact the undersigned...
Please find enclosed herewith...
I should be obliged if...
Attached herein is a copy of the aforementioned deed...

And, of course, the classic:

If there is anything further I can do to help, please do not hesitate to contact me.

Trust me, expressions like these are outdated and unnecessary. Cut them out.

MAY, MIGHT OR CAN?

Are you unsure about whether to use can, may or might? Their meaning is subtly different. Can means capable of, may asks permission or shows possibility when an outcome is unknown, and might (which is the past tense form of may) is used to refer to something that was likely or possible at some point in the past.

So, if you were asking permission to go to the park, the correct way would be to say 'may I go to the park?' It would be incorrect to say 'can I go to the park?'

Examples:

If I hadn't flunked the interview, I may have got the job. ✗

If I hadn't flunked the interview, I might have got the job. ✓

I might start my diet tomorrow. ✗

I may start my diet tomorrow. ✓

Don't worry if you don't always get it right. People are far more relaxed about language these days and 'may', 'might' and 'can' are becoming increasingly interchangeable.

N

NOUNS

A noun is a name. It can be the name of a person, a place, an object, an animal—the name of anything at all.

Examples:

Person: *Mother, teacher, Mozart, Jane.*
Place: *house, France, avenue, Madrid, kitchen.*
Object: *table, sofa, flower, raindrop, plate, apple.*
Animal: *dog, cat, rhinoceros, terrier.*

Pronouns are words used to refer to other specific nouns. The most common English pronouns include he, she, me, I, us, we, you, it they and them.

Abstract nouns are ideas and qualities that are abstract or theoretical—things and emotions that you can't see, hear, taste or touch.

Examples:

Love, religion, bravery, impatience, skill, friendship.

Common nouns are the general names given to objects or members of a group. Proper nouns are more specific because they identify a particular place, person or thing. Most proper nouns begin with a capital letter.

Examples:

Common noun	Proper noun
country	Canada
car	Aston Martin
city	Liverpool
month	October
day	Wednesday
entrepreneur	Bill Gates
saint	St David

Collective nouns are words that define a group of objects. For instance, you could have a *cast* of actors, a *host* of angels, or a *pack* of hounds.

In fact, there is a whole subset of interesting collective nouns that describe different groups of animals. Here are just a few:

A <u>colony</u> of bats *A <u>murder</u> of crows*
A <u>parliament</u> of owls *A <u>pod</u> of porpoises*
An <u>unkindness</u> of ravens *A <u>nest</u> of vipers*
A <u>school</u> of whales *A <u>business</u> of ferrets*
A <u>swarm</u> of bees *An <u>ostentation</u> of peacocks*
A <u>congregation</u> of alligators *A <u>bed</u> of clams*

Some of these collective nouns vary. For instance, you'd refer to a group of geese on the ground or on water as a *gaggle of geese*, but if they were flying over your head it would be a *skein of geese.*

And for the final word on nouns, remember that groups such as a government, a party, a family, a team, a company, or a country are all **singular nouns.** If you refer to the group as a whole, use a singular verb.

Examples:

*The team **is** improving efficiency.*

*The company **was** in financial difficulties.*

NUMBERS

Here are a few things to remember when including numbers in your text:

- Write one to nine in words and 10 or over in figures. There are exceptions to this: such as when you write someone's age *(Jill was 7 years old and Jack was 12)*, when you're referring to things like school years *(the children were all in Year 7 at school)*, or when you mention statistics *(8% of customers were aged 60)*.

- Use a comma when you write large numbers: *2,500 or 87,883.*

- Avoid starting a sentence with a number. When you have no choice, write it out as a word: *Twelve of the cars were parked illegally.*

- Money should always be written in figures, such as *£12.48.* There's no need to include 'p' if you start with a £ sign, but if the amount is less than £1, add a 'p' at the end, as in *35p.*

- Weights and volumes are also best written in figures: *125gm* or *5ml.*

- If you're numbering lists or sections of your document, it's clearer if you use Arabic numbers, not Roman numerals. In other words, use 3, not iii, and 7 instead of VII.

NEITHER AND NOR

'Neither' and 'nor' should be used together, and 'or' goes with 'either'. So, you'd say: *Neither Nell nor Jane can go to the party* and *either Jack or Bridget will go instead.*

ORDER

When you're writing about order, apply the same rules you would use for writing numbers.

Example: First, second, third through to ninth in words, then *10th, 12th, 15th , 22nd* and so on.

OTT

When you're trying to persuade your customers to buy your product or service, it's easy to be over enthusiastic, especially if you're writing a marketing leaflet or promotional flyer. Avoid using phrases like this:

- *exciting new service*
- *amazing performance*
- *excellent product*
- *fabulous offer.*

Or, in the words of a company promoting a weight loss product, *the finest fat burner ever!!!*

You should leave it up to your customers to decide whether something is exciting, amazing or fabulous—and be very careful about claiming that your product is 'the finest ever', unless, of course, you can prove it. Exaggerating for effect—known as hyperbole—screams 'sales pitch'. If you want to persuade your customers to buy your product, it's much better to write briefly about the product's *features* and then concentrate on how the product will *benefit* the customer you're hoping will buy from you.

Example:

This new service means you can now access your account online, so you can make payments at any time of the day or night, whenever it's convenient for you.

P

PUNCTUATION

When we read a document or a book, we scarcely notice the punctuation and yet, without it, words would blend together chaotically. Punctuation marks give a sentence organisation and structure, helping us to clarify its meaning.

You've probably heard the joke about the teacher who wrote *woman without her man is nothing* on a blackboard and asked his class to punctuate the sentence correctly. The story goes that the boys all wrote *Woman, without her man, is nothing*. Whereas the girls in the class opted for *Woman: without her, man is nothing*. Ok, maybe not one of the world's funniest jokes, but it shows how altering punctuation can totally change the meaning of a sentence.

So let's concentrate on punctuation for a while. In this section we'll take a look at full stops, commas, colons and semicolons (other punctuation marks such as question marks, exclamation marks and quotation marks are covered elsewhere in this book, as are hyphens, ellipsis and apostrophes).

Full stops mark the end of a sentence. Most of us understand how to use them properly, but it's easy to slip up. If we do, we'll end up with a long rambling sentence held together by nothing more than a comma.

Example:

The council's decision to close down its cottage hospital has caused an outcry, a petition has been signed by 854 local people who are concerned about getting convenient access to outpatient treatment. ✗

This sentence contains two distinct statements, which should be separated by a full stop.

The council's decision to close down its cottage hospital has caused an outcry. A petition has been signed by 854 local people who are concerned about getting convenient access to outpatient treatment. ✓

Commas are more subtle than full stops and, for that reason, can be tricky to get to grips with. Commas have many purposes, including listing or itemising words, setting names apart (or bracketing them). They're also used to emphasise words.

Examples:

Listing or itemising: *The bakery sold bread, pies, pastries and cakes.*
Bracketing: *The cupcakes, which are iced and decorated, always sell very quickly.*
Setting apart names: *To be honest, Ted, I really don't like pork pies.*
For emphasis: *I will pay you for it, of course.*

Use commas between adjectives in a sentence if the adjectives define separate attributes. If the adjectives work together to form a single image, commas aren't needed. This is probably best explained with some examples:

Examples:

The crowd chanted in loud, angry, intimidating voices.

The adjectives in this sentence describe different features of the voices that are chanting, and so need to be separated by commas.

She lived in a large half-timbered thatched cottage.

The adjectives here work together to build an overall picture of the cottage, so commas aren't necessary.

Semicolons are used mainly to join two complete sentences into a single sentence when:

- They are not connected by a word such as 'and' or 'but' that would require a comma.
- The two sentences are too closely connected to be separated by a full stop.

Examples:

Ted didn't like pork pies; not at all.

Ten horses began the race; only four are still running.

The last example could also be written as:

Ten horses began the race, but only four are still running.

Colons have many uses. They can introduce a list, present a conclusion or example, and introduce questions or quotations.

Examples:

Introducing a list: *Helen took in the scene: broken fences, smashed windows, and a old settee in the back yard.*

Presenting a conclusion: *The plant was clearly dying: its leaves were yellow and withered.*

Introducing a question: *The question was this: would she be able to afford the insurance if she bought the car?*

Introducing a quotation: *The teacher closed the book and looked at her class: "Who can tell me what the poem means?" she asked.*

PROOF READING

If there's time, it's always a good idea to get someone else to check your work, especially if you're producing a document or leaflet that will be distributed widely. A fresh pair of eyes will soon spot any errors that you've missed.

When you're writing you can often become blind to the words on the page. It's easy to read what you think you've written, rather than what's actually there. That's why it's essential to thoroughly proof read your document.

One of the best ways to proof read is to print out a copy of the final draft of your work. It's easier to spot mistakes on paper than when you're reading a document on-screen. With a paper copy, you can also scribble notes and changes in the margin.

Try to do your proof reading somewhere quiet like an empty meeting room. Getting away from ringing phones and chatty colleagues will help you focus on the task in hand. It will also give you an opportunity to read your work out loud if you want to. This can help you pick up on misplaced commas and missing words, and highlight awkwardly constructed or over-long sentences.

Proofreading may seem tedious and boring, but it's the only way to find and correct errors before your work is published.

PASSIVE SENTENCES

You can see the difference between writing in an active voice and a passive voice in the examples below.

Examples:

(**Active**): *The soldier received a commendation.*

(**Passive**): *A commendation was received by the soldier.*

(**Active**): *His wife drove the car.*

(**Passive**): *The car was driven by his wife.*

Writing passively can make your writing sound dull, clumsy and even bureaucratic. Passive writing also uses more words than active sentences and has less energy and power. The active voice gives more of a sense of urgency and vigour. Read the two examples below and decide for yourself which works best:

Example:

(**Passive**): *A high demand for the service was shown by the research.*

(**Active**): *The research showed a high demand for the service.*

QUOTATION MARKS

Use quotation marks to enclose any direct speech you're reporting in a document or press release.

Examples:

"This new facility will help us to cut costs and provide a better service for our online customers," said John Smith, Managing Director at ABC Company.

"I won't sign the contract," Helen said, "unless you remove the last clause.

When the quotation runs on to more than one paragraph, put a quotation mark at the beginning of each paragraph and at the end of the final paragraph.

Some people choose to use single, rather than double

quotation marks. Double quotation marks are usually the preferred option in the UK, but either double or single marks are acceptable, as long as you're consistent. Decide on a 'house style' and stick to it.

If you include a quote within a quote, use single quotation marks if you're using doubles for your main quotation, or doubles if your main quotation uses singles—see the examples below.

Examples:

"We're providing this service in response to our customers who are always saying: 'Give us more ways of paying online'. At ABC we always listen to customer feedback," John Smith added.

or

'We're providing this service in response to our customers who are always saying: "Give us more ways of paying online". At ABC we always listen to customer feedback,' John Smith added.

Quotation marks are also used for emphasis or to show when a word has a special meaning, or is a misnomer.

Examples:

The 'real' diamond in the necklace was nothing more than a piece of badly cut glass.

She claimed she was an 'expert'.

Quotation marks vary in shape, depending on which font you use. If you're using them to show speech or dialogue, choose quotation marks that are 'tadpole' shaped (like this ' ' or " "). You should use what are called prime and double prime symbols to describe feet and inches or minutes and seconds. These are straighter symbols that look like this ′ and ″. In Microsoft Word you can add these using the insert 'symbol' function. Or, choose a font that includes straight quotation marks, such as Verdana or Tahoma.

Examples:

Tom was 6' 2" ✗ (These quotation marks are created using the font Garamond).

Tom was 6′ 2″ ✓ (Here, the prime and double prime symbols are shown using the Verdana font).

QUESTION MARKS

How often do you forget to use these to mark the end of a question? It's an easy mistake to make, so be sure to look out for any that you've missed when you're proof reading your document.

You only need a question mark when you're asking a direct question. If your sentence asks an indirect question, a question mark isn't necessary.

Example:

(**Direct question**): *Will you have dinner with me?*

(**Indirect question**): *He asked her if she'd have dinner with him.*

R

READER

The most important thing to ask yourself before you start writing is: *'Who am I writing for?'* Writing a sales letter to a customer will be very different to producing a technical report for a business audience. You should adjust your writing style to suit your *reader.* Try to keep it as simple as possible, even if you're writing about something complicated.

To be effective it helps to be clear about the message you want to communicate and understand why you're writing—is it to inform, advise or persuade?

Taking a few moments to think about your message and plan your document will help you choose the best writing style for your audience and help you communicate successfully.

REPETITION

Once you've finished writing, read through your text, looking out for sentences or paragraphs where you've repeated information or the same word twice or more. If you find that a word is cropping up too often, replace it with something else if you can, or rephrase the sentence completely if you have to.

Example:

The aim of the report was to report on how new products were being developed in response to emerging technologies and the changing needs of customers. The report also took into account the changing economic climate.

The repeated words in this sentence are *report* and *changing*. Here's how you could make changes to avoid word repetition:

The aim of the report was to describe how new products were being developed in response to emerging technologies and the changing needs of customers. The report also took into account the recent economic downturn .

S

SPELLING

Always check your spelling. The quickest way is to use the spell checker on your word processor, but remember that this won't pick up the incorrect use of words if they are spelt correctly. For example, your spell checker wouldn't pick up the fact that you'd typed *there* instead of *their*.

It's amazing how many of your customers will notice a spelling mistake in a letter you've sent them. Spelling errors make you and your organisation look unprofessional. If there's time, ask a colleague to proof read your document or, at the very least, read it through at least once yourself.

If you have problems remembering how to spell a word, try breaking it up into smaller parts and learn each part separately. You can also try using mnemonics to help you remember the words you have trouble with.

A mnemonic is a learning technique or device to help you remember things.

Examples:

Lots of people mix up the words *stationery* (meaning writing materials) and *stationary* (meaning motionless). A good mnemonic for this is to remember 'e' for envelope. That way you know that the spelling for station<u>e</u>ry (as in envelopes and other writing materials) has an 'e' in it.

To remember how to spell the word *rhythm,* remember the mnemonic *<u>r</u>hythm <u>h</u>as <u>y</u>our <u>t</u>wo <u>h</u>ips <u>m</u>oving*.

To make sure you spell *accommodation* correctly (with two 'c's and two 'm's), think of two mismatched people called <u>C</u>heerful <u>C</u>harlie and <u>M</u>iserable <u>M</u>ike living together in a house.

Necessary often trips people up. Do you wonder whether it's two 'c's and two 's's... two 'c's and one 's'? Well, there's a traditional mnemonic for this one that's easy to memorise. *It is necessary to have <u>one</u> <u>c</u>ollar and <u>two</u> <u>s</u>ocks*. One 'c' and two 's's.

Separate is another tricky one to get right. Lots of people spell it as *seperate*, but with the mnemonic *sep<u>a</u>r<u>a</u>te* has '*a rat*' in it, you need never get it wrong again.

SAY IT SIMPLY

Try to help your reader by choosing words that are easy to understand. Replace long or complicated words with simple alternatives.

Difficult	Easy	Difficult	Easy
additionally	also / and	endeavour	try
adequate	enough	enquire	ask
adjacent	next to	frequently	often
assist	help	in excess of	more than
attempt	try	in the event of	if
commence	start / begin	per annum	a year
completion	end	prior to	before
concerning	about	subsequently	later
demonstrate	show	terminate	end
due to the fact	because	utilise	use

You get the idea. If you've used a word that's a bit long winded, change it. Refer to a thesaurus, or use your word processor's in-built thesaurus. In Microsoft Word all you have to do is double-click the word you want to look up, hold down shift and press F7 and a list of alternative words will pop up on the right hand side of your screen. You can also refer to the *Writing at Work* list of Everyday Words on page 105.

T

TAUTOLOGY

Tautologies are words that repeat the same thing. Check your text and see how many unnecessary words you can cut out.

Examples:

Claim your <u>free gift</u>.

She had recently given birth to a <u>pair of twins</u>.

He made <u>brief notes</u> about his future plans.

In most cases you can correct the tautology by removing the unnecessary words:

Claim your gift.

She had recently given birth to twins.

He made notes about his plans.

TONE OF VOICE

The tone of voice you adopt in your writing should reflect the nature of the document, who you're writing to, the kind of organisation you work for, and the products you sell. A company selling colourful beachwear will adopt a different tone of voice in its promotional literature to one selling medical equipment. Your tone will also vary depending on whether you're writing to a customer to let them know about your latest product, or composing a warning letter to an employee about their poor timekeeping.

No matter what your reason for writing, try to be honest and tactful. If the situation requires you to be firm or critical, try to do so without being sarcastic or unnecessarily harsh. Remember that people interpret words in different ways, so tread carefully and make sure you select words that are appropriate and right for the situation you're writing about.

Being positive and upbeat is more likely to get the result you want. When you're writing to your customers avoid being too business like, as this can come across as cold. If your message is positive or routine, adopt a warm and friendly approach by using 'you', 'your' and 'us' (see page 99). However, if you're in disagreement with the person you're writing to, or you are disciplining an employee, I'd advise you to be more formal.

TITLES

When you abbreviate titles, they're easier to read if you don't use full stops. The same applies to shortened words, such as street, avenue, Limited and Association.

Examples:

- Rev
- Mr
- Mrs
- Dr
- St
- Ave
- Ltd
- Assoc

TIME

The clearest way to show times in your text and on signs and posters is to show them without noughts and with no space between the time and the am and pm. For example, instead of **9.00am to 7.00pm**, it's simpler to write **9am to 7pm**. Use 12noon when you're referring to midday.

Avoid referring to the 24-hour clock because some people find this confusing. It's better to say 7.15pm than 19.15.

A 24 hour clock does have a place in some businesses though. Bus and train companies often use this method to display timetables to clearly distinguish between morning, afternoon and evening services.

U

UNNECESSARY WORDS

If you find you've littered your sentences with unnecessary words and phrases, cut them out. I've already mentioned the old chestnut that many people still use to bring their letters to a conclusion: *If there is anything further I can do to assist, please do not hesitate to contact me.* That's 17 words! Why not say: *If you need any further help, call me on 01234 567891* instead? That's six words fewer and it includes a call to action.

V

VOCABULARY

You can really improve your writing by expanding your vocabulary. There are lots of ways to do this. Regular reading helps. Keep a dictionary nearby, and when you're working through a document, book or newspaper and come across a word you're not familiar with, look it up.

Lots of words have similar meanings (or synonyms) but each one will have a slightly different focus or emphasis. Finding exactly the right word to describe what you want to say can be really satisfying, so it's worth trying a few variations if you have time. You'll find this easier to do if you have a wide vocabulary.

VERIFICATION

If you're putting together a document or leaflet, make sure you verify your facts and figures before sending it to print. It's particularly important to check times and dates if you're advertising an event or a meeting. Is 7 January 2012 really a Friday? Is the meeting scheduled to start at 1pm or 2pm? If your report or newsletter refers to further information on another page, check that you've referred your reader to the right page number.

All of these checks are part of a thorough proofing of the text. Never take anything for granted.

VERBS

Verbs are words that put action into sentences and make them do something.

Examples:

To talk • talking • talked
To write • writing • wrote
To laugh • laughing • laughed
To eat • eating • ate

There are a number of words where the verb can easily be confused with the noun, including:

Advice (noun): *She took his advice and read the document.*

Advise (verb): *'I would advise that you read the document.'*

Effect (noun): *The trainee doctors studied the effects of obesity.*

Affect (verb): *Protests to the referee did not affect his decision.*

Licence (noun): *You will need a current driving licence for the job.*

License (verb): *The magistrate decided not to license the restaurant to sell alcohol.*

Practice (noun): *She ran her own dental practice.*

Practise (verb): *She decided to practise to improve her skills.*

WEBSITES

Writing website content requires a different approach to writing letters, reports or marketing materials. Web users rarely read web pages in full. Instead they scan the page and pick out certain words or sentences, so ideally you should keep your word count to about half of what you'd use in printed materials.

Useful tools for web writing include highlighting key words by making them hyperlinks to other pages or sites, putting them into **bold** font, or making them subheadings. Subheadings will help you break the text into short paragraphs that contain one key message. Bullet points are also useful for lists.

Include the most important facts at the top of the web page in the first few lines of text. That way, when someone scans your page, they're more likely to take in the key messages and contact details you've included in the opening lines. It also means that anyone with a visual impairment who is using a screen reader will be able to access important information quickly.

If you're asked to put a website together or write content for web pages, it's worth reading a good guide to writing for the web before you start (see Further Reading on page 129). If you sell products on your website, you'll take a different approach to someone writing content for a site that's purely information based. Either way, there are a whole set of rules that apply to writing and structuring content for websites, so it's worth spending some time researching the subject before you begin.

WHO OR WHOM?

'Who' is a subject pronoun and 'whom' is an object pronoun. To use these words correctly, you have to keep them in their proper places. The best way to check if they're where they should be is to match them against related subject and object pronouns:

Match '*who*' with *she, he, they* and *we*.

'*Whom*' matches with *her, him, them* and *us*.

Once you understand this matching process, it's easy to check whether you are using 'who' or 'whom' properly.

Examples:

Who will it be? (Will it be he? Will it be they?) ✗

Whom will it be? (Will it be him? Will it be them?) ✓

Whom do you think is winning? (Do you think him is winning?) ✗

Who do you think is winning? (Do you think he is winning?) ✓

Who is that woman? (Who is she?) ✓

Whom is that woman? (Who is her?) ✗

The men, four of whom were wearing hats, entered the room. (The men entered the room. Four of them were wearing hats.) ✓

The men, four of who were wearing hats, entered the room. (The men entered the room. Four of they were wearing hats.) ✗

Who is at the door? (Is he at the door?) ✔

Whom is at the door? (Is him at the door?) ✗

Whom did you see at the door? (Did you see her at the door?) ✔

Who did you see at the door? (Did you see she at the door?) ✗

In the last examples, the subject of the sentence *'who is at the door?'* is *'who'*. In the sentence *'whom did you see at the door?'* the subject is *'you'* and the object is *'whom'*.

When in doubt about whether to use who or whom, think about this matching process and you'll soon be able to decide which one to choose.

WHICH OR THAT?

Over the last few decades, 'which' and 'that' have become pretty much interchangeable, but they are subtly different. Strictly speaking, there are rules about how they should be used.

'*That*' introduces essential information that defines the meaning of a preceding clause. '*Which*' provides extra information to a sentence where defining information has already been provided.

Examples:

On its new website, the supermarket is offering a service that is ideal for busy people who prefer to do their shopping online.

The supermarket is offering a new service, HomeShop, which is ideal for busy people who prefer to do their shopping online.

WHAT, WHEN, WHERE, WHY, WHO

You should think carefully about these five words when you're planning your text.

Example:

If you were drafting a marketing leaflet to launch a new product you would need to consider:

<u>**What**</u> are the features of your new product?
<u>**What**</u> do you want your leaflet to achieve?
<u>**Why**</u> is your product important to your cutomers?
<u>**Where**</u> can your customers buy the product?
<u>**Who**</u> are your customers? Are they already familiar with your company – if not, explain <u>**who**</u> you are.
<u>**When**</u> will the product be available?

Remembering the five Ws—what, why, where, who and when—will help you pull together all of the information you need for your document, no matter what it is you're writing about.

EXCLAMATION MARKS

Ok, I know exclamation begins with an 'E'—but I couldn't think of anything else to write about for the letter X!

Exclamation marks at the end of a sentence are used to show surprise, emphasis and tone of voice, but use them sparingly. Don't fall into the trap of adding them in to make things sound more exciting than they really are. Too many exclamation marks in a text can be irritating and distracting. Especially if you use more than one!!!

Reserve exclamation marks for quotes to show someone expressing emotion. If you've run a competition on your website and you're quoting the winner's response, you could say something like: 'When I heard the news I couldn't believe it! I've never won anything before.'

YOU, YOUR

Addressing your audience directly can really improve the effectiveness of your writing. Whether you're writing to a customer, a colleague or another company, frequent use of 'I', 'we' and 'you' in your sentences will make your letter or document less formal and far more personal. This will make the reader feel they're being addressed individually and help them to identify with what you're saying. Once you've established this style, make sure you keep it going throughout the text.

Z

ZZZzzz

Don't send your reader to sleep... don't be boring and don't go on too long. Hold the reader's interest by making every sentence count and avoid waffling. Keep your sentences short and get to the point quickly, but be wary of using phrases that sound like shorthand. For instance, rather than saying something like 'service delivery' it's much better to say 'the delivery of services', even though it does use a few more words.

In business writing, less is more. Busy people haven't got time to read unnecessarily long documents. Keep your word count to a minimum, but make sure the words you do use are the right ones to communicate all of your key messages. And, on that point, I'll end (don't want to send you to sleep).

Writing at Work

A List of Everyday Words

A	
(hold in) abeyance	wait, postpone
abscond	flee, escape, run away
absence (of)	no, none
abundance	a lot of, enough, plenty
accede to	allow, agree to
accentuate	emphasise, stress, highlight
accommodation	housing, home, property
accompany	go with, go along with
accomplish	do, complete, achieve
(in) accordance	in line with, because of
accordingly	so, for that reason
accurate	correct, right
acknowledge	accept, admit
acknowledge receipt	thank you for
acquaint (yourself)	find out
acquiesce	accept, agree
acquire	get, get hold of, buy
actioned	done, carried out

additional	further, more, extra
additionally	also, and
adequate	enough
adjacent	next to, nearby
adjust	change
administer	manage, run, look after
admissible	acceptable, allowable
(in) advance	before
advantageous	useful, helpful, valuable
affix	fix to, attach
aforesaid	earlier in this document
albeit	even though
alleviate	ease, lessen
allocate	share, give, hand out
alternative	other, different
ameliorate	improve, make better
amendment	change
anticipate	expect, predict
apparent	clear, obvious, plain

appreciable	large, great
apprise	tell, inform
appropriate	right, suitable, proper
approximately	around, about, roughly
ascertain	find out, learn, discover
assemble	gather, build
assist / assistance	help, support
attempt	try
attend	join, go to, be at
authorise	allow, let
authority	right, power
axiomatic	obvious, goes without saying

B	
backdate	from, make earlier
belated	late
beneficial	useful, helpful, of value
bestow	give, award, grant
breach	break

C

calculate	work out, add up
cease	stop, end, finish
circumvent	get around, avoid
clarify	explain, make clear
combine	mix, merge, join
commence	begin, start
commensurate	equal to
competent	can, able
compile	gather, collect, put together
completion	end, close
comply with	meet the terms, keep to
component	part
comprising	including, involving
compulsory	required, necessary, must
conceal	hide, cover up
concerning	about
conclusion	decision, end
concur	agree, accept

condition	requirement, you must
confer	give, consult, compare views
(in) conjunction with	and, with
consecutive days	days in a row
consent	agree to
consequently	so, as a result
considerable	large, great
consists of	made up of
constitute	form, make up
construct	make, build
construe	interpret, taken to mean
consumed	used, eaten
contemplate	think about, consider
contrary to	against
contravenes	breaks, goes against
(when) convenient	when you can
convert	change
convey or convey to	carry or tell
correspond	write, contact

corroborate	back up, support, prove
criteria	conditions, standards
cumulative	added together
currently	now
customary	usual, normal, ordinary

D	
decrease	go down, drop, cut
deduct	take off, take away, remove
deem	view as, consider, believe
defer	delay, put off
deficiency	lack of, shortage
delete	cross out, remove
demonstrate	show, explain, prove
denote	mean, show
depart	leave
depict	show, describe
designate	appoint, choose
despatch	send, post

despite	although, even though
detach	tear off
deteriorate	get worse, worsen
determine	find out, work out, decide
detrimental	harmful, damaging
diminish	reduce, lessen, weaken
disburse	pay, pay out, distribute
discharge (duties)	carry out
disclose	tell
disconnect	cut off
discontinue	end, stop, withdraw
discrete	separate, distinct
discreet	tactful
discuss	talk about
dispose of	get rid of
disseminate	spread, publicise
domiciled in	living in
dominant	leading, main
donate	give

due to	because
duration	time
dwelling	home, house, property

E	
earnings	wages, money coming in
economical	good value, cheap
elect	pick, choose, decide on
eligible	qualified, allowed
elucidate	explain, spell out, make clear
emoluments	wages, money, income
emphasise	stress, highlight
employment	work, job
empower	allow, let
enable	allow
enclosed	inside, here is, with this
encounter	meet
endeavour	try
enquire	ask

ensure	make sure, make certain
entitlement	right
envisage	expect, imagine, see
equitable	fair
equivalent	equal to, the same as
erroneous	wrong, incorrect
establish	show, find out, set up, begin
estimate	work out, expected cost
evaluate	assess, check, test, value
(in the) event of	if
evident	clear, plain, obvious
evince	show, display
examine	check, look at
(in) excess of	more than
excessive	too many, too much
exclude	leave out
exclusively	only
exempt from	free from
expedite	rush, speed up, hurry

expeditiously	as soon as possible
expenditure	costs, spending
expire	run out, end, finish
extant	existing, in force
extremity	limit

F	
fabricate	make, make up, invent, fake
facilitate	help, assist, make possible
factor	reason, feature, thing
failure to	if you don't
feasible	possible, practical, likely
forfeit	give up, lose
formulate	plan, put together
forthwith	now, at once, straight away
forward	send, send on
frequently	often
furnish	give, provide
furthermore	also, and, in addition

G	
generate	create, produce, give, make
grant	allow, award, funding
gratuity	tip
guidance	help, advice, support

H	
henceforth	in future, from now on
hereby	now (or delete the word)
herein	here, in this
hereinafter	after this
hereof	of this
hereto	to this
heretofore	until now, previously
hereunder	below
herewith	with this
hierarchy	order, organisation
hitherto	so far, until now
hybrid	cross, mixture, mix

I

identical	the same as
illustrate	show, explain
immediately	at once, now, straight away
impart	tell, inform, pass on
implement	carry out, do, put in place
imply	suggest, hint at
inadequate	not enough, poor, too little
inappropriate	wrong, unsuitable
incapable of	unable to
incapacitated	ill, sick, unwell, unfit
inception	start, beginning, launch
incorporating	including, featuring
increment	increase, step, pay rise
indicate	show, suggest
infirmity	illness
inform	tell, let know
infrequently	not often, from time to time
initially	firstly, to begin with

initiate	begin, start
in lieu of	instead of
insert	put in
inspect	check, look at
instances	cases, examples
intend to	will, plan to, aim to, mean to
interim	temporary, acting
intimate	say, hint
irrespective of	despite, even if
issue	send, give

J	
jeopardise	put at risk, threaten

K	
keynote (speech)	important, defining, central

L	
legislation	law

liable	you must, have to, responsible
liaise (with)	meet, discuss, work (with)
locality	place, area
locate	find, put

M

magnitude	size, scale, importance
maintained	kept, repaired
maintenance	upkeep, care
mandatory	required, (you) must
manner	way
manufacture	make
marginal	small, slight
materialise	appear, happen
merchandise	goods, products, stock
miscellaneous	other, mixed, various
mislay	lose
modify	change, adjust
moreover	also, and, as well

N	
necessitates	has to, needs, calls for
negligent	careless
negligible	very small, tiny
nevertheless	yet, but, however, even so
nonetheless	even so, however, yet
notify	inform, tell, let know
notwithstanding	even if, despite, all the same
numerous	many, several

O	
objective	aim, goal, purpose
(it is) obligatory	(you) must, required
observe	watch, study
obsolete	old, out-of-date
obtain	get, receive
occupation	job
occur	happen
operate	work, run

optimum	best, peak, ideal
option	choice, possibility
ordinarily	usually, normally, in general
otherwise	or else, if not
outstanding (bill)	unpaid, due
overall	total, whole
owing to	because of

P	
partially	partly, in part
participate	take part, join in, get involved
particulars	details, facts
pending	until, incomplete, awaiting
per annum	a year
perform	do, complete, carry out
permissible	allowable, allowed
permit	let, allow
personnel	staff, workers, employees
persons	people, anyone

peruse	read, look at
portion	part, share, piece
possess	own, have
possessions	belongings
practically	almost, nearly
preceding month	month before
predominant	main, major
prescribe	set, fix
preserve	keep, protect, save
previous	earlier, before
principal	main, chief, most important
principle	theory, rule, value
prior to	before
proceed	continue, go on
procure	get, buy
profusion	plenty, large amount, lots
prohibit	ban, stop
projected	likely, estimated
prolonged	long, lengthy, drawn-out

promptly	quickly, at once, on time
promulgate	advertise, circulate, announce
proportion	amount, share, part
provide	give, offer
provided that	as long as, if
provisional	for now, temporary
provisions	rules, terms, supplies
proximity	closeness, nearness
purchase	buy
purport	claim, seem
pursuant to	under, because of

Q

qualify (for)	can get, be able to get

R

receive	get
reconsider	think again, go back over
reduce	cut, lower

reduction	cut, saving, discount
refer to	talk about, mention
regarding	about, on
regret	sorry
regulation	rule
reimburse	repay, pay back, refund
reiterate	repeat, say again, go over
relating to	about
relinquish	give up
remain	stay
remainder	the rest, what's left
remit	send, pay
remittance	payment
remuneration	pay, wages salary, fee
render	make, give, send
renew (your claim)	claim again
represent	show, stand for, be
request	ask, question
require	need, want, call for

requirements	needs, rules
reside	live
residence	house, home, where you live
response	answer
(a) responsibility to	you must, should
restriction	limit
resume	begin again, restart, continue
retain	keep, hold on to
revenue	income, money, profit
reverse (of)	back of
review	reread, look at again
revised	new, changed, updated

S	
safeguard	protect, look after
salary	pay
scrutinise	study, check
select	pick, choose
settle	pay

settlement	payment
shortly	soon
signage	sign, notice, poster
significant	important
similarly	also, in the same way
solely	only
specific	exact, particular
state	say, tell, write down
statutory	legal, by law
stipulate	say, instruct
subject to	depending on, bound by
submit	send, give
subsequent to	after
subsequently	later, then
substantial	large, big, a lot of
sufficient	enough
supplement	go with, add to, extra
supplementary	extra, added, more
supply	give, sell, deliver

suspend	put on hold, stop for now
systematic	organised

T	
tabulate	chart, arrange
takeover	buy out
tangible	real, solid, definite
technology	equipment, know-how, tools
terminate	end, finish, stop
thereafter	afterwards, then
thereby	so, in that way, because of
therefore	for this reason, as a result
therein	in that, there
thereof	of that
thereto	to that
thus	so, as a result
transfer	move
transmit	send
transpired	became known, happened

U	
ultimately	in the end, finally
unable to	can't
unavailability	lack of, absence
undernoted	the following
undersigned	I, we
understated	modest, low-key
undertake	take on, agree to, promise, do
uniform	same, similar, alike
unilateral	one-sided
unoccupied	empty, vacant
utilise	use

V	
variation	change, difference
vendor	seller
verify	confirm, prove, check
(in the) vicinity	near, nearby, in the area
virtually	almost, nearly

visualise	picture, imagine, see, predict
vocation	job, career, calling

W	
waive	ignore, give up, not claim
whatsoever	whatever, at all, of any kind
whensoever	when
whereas	but, while
whether	if
wilfully	deliberately
withhold	refuse, hold back
wholly	all, completely, fully, totally

Y	
yield	give up, profit, return

Z	
zone	area, region

FURTHER READING

We hope this quick and easy guide has whetted your appetite for the English language. If you'd like to read more about grammar and language, try these:

Oxford A-Z of Grammar and Punctuation by John Seely —published by OUP Oxford ISBN 9780199564675

Concise Oxford English Dictionary: Main Edition—published by OUP Oxford ISBN 9780199601080

Oxford Guide to Plain English by Martin Cutts— published by OUP Oxford ISBN 9780199558506

Collins Improve Your Grammar by Graham King— published by Collins ISBN 9780007288083

Collins Complete Writing Guide by Graham King— published by Collins ISBN 9780007288076

The Elements of Style by William Strunk Jr & E B White —published by Longman ISBN 9780205309023

Troublesome Words by Bill Bryson—published by Penguin ISBN 9780141040394

The State of the Language: English Observed by Philip Howard — published by Penguin ISBN 9780140080865 (currently out of print).

Writing for the Web—published by Chambers ISBN 9780550103246

INDEX

About the author

Ellis Morgan has worked as a professional communicator for 20 years in both the public and private sectors. She has experience of customer communications in the railway and education sectors and, more recently, in local government. Her roles have included editor and copywriter for newsletters and customer magazines, website content author, and writer of press releases and leaflets. She has also delivered training and staff workshops on writing in plain English and, in her spare time, has had articles and short fiction published as a freelance writer.